The Immigrant:

How to Land Your Next 6 Figure Dream Job in the United States

Author: Li Lin

Contributing Authors:

Esther Howard, Queenie Johnson, Karen Kartika, Ivanna Kujanovic, Ankita Maini, Margaret Olatunbosun, Albert Qian, Lionnel Yamentou, Peng Zhang

Copyright © 2016 Li Lin

All rights reserved.

ISBN:1535406615
ISBN-13: 978-1535406611

DEDICATION

Dedicated to all the hard working and ambitious immigrants around the world who inspire me every day.

TABLE OF CONTENTS

	Acknowledgments	i
Chapter 1	Who this Book is For	1
Chapter 2	How to Make it in America	6
Chapter 3	Succeeding in the US from Age 0-100	17
Chapter 4	Finding the Right Job for You	25
Chapter 5	The Only 2 Things That Matter in the Job Search	32
Chapter 6	Creating a Network from Nothing	36
Chapter 7	Acing Job Interviews Like a Rock Star	43
Chapter 8	How to Make $100,000+ a Year	53
Chapter 9	Job Tales from Professionals Around the World	64
Chapter 10	How to Land Your American Dream Job	101

ACKNOWLEDGMENTS

Thank you to all the amazing contributors who have shared their job tales around the world.

Thank you Esther for sharing your story of how you became a software engineer.

Thank you Queenie for being one of the most charismatic teachers I know.

Thank you Karen for inspiring me with your story and teaching me about your country.

Thank you Ivanna for being the first to jump on this project, and I hope that your language skills may rub off on me one day.

Thank you Ankita, for being the TOEFL expert in this book, which is so needed for immigrants in the US.

Thank you Margaret for being so funny all the time and your unparalleled work ethic inspires me so much.

Thank you Albert for creating Albert's list, thank you for referring clients to me and I am sure I will continue paying you commission for many years to come.

Thank you Lionnel for being such a great Meetup leader and giving me an opportunities to speak to your students, you are a true great leader.

Thank you Peng for creating a resource for H-1B and OPT seeking students, it is a beautiful site that has helped many.

Thank you to all of my clients who have worked with me, shared with me their amazing stories, and who are now in their dream jobs & dream companies!

CHAPTER 1: WHO THIS BOOK IS FOR

This book took me 16 years to write.

16 years ago I didn't know any English.

16 years ago I was still in Shanghai, China.

It took me 16 years to learn *what it's like to be an immigrant in the US*, which included the following:

Overcoming the language barrier:

I didn't know any English--I only knew how to nod and shake my head.

My identity as a student who barely studied and still got great grades was destroyed overnight.

There was no ESL program at my school and I was the only immigrant, so I was held back a grade.

While my peers could just watch a movie and write the book report, I remember reading the book *Island of the Blue Dolphins* cover to cover 3 times, and still had no idea what the book was about.

But I was determined to learn English, and because it was do or die time, I was able to graduate my high school senior year as the top

4% of my class and went onto graduate from UC Berkeley in 2012.

Learning What It's Like to Be a Foreigner:

More than the language barrier, I had to learn American culture, what's cool, and what's definitely not.

Be the first in the family to do (fill in the blank):

As an immigrant, most of the time you will be expected to help family members who are older or came to the US later.

It's a fine line to balance between feeling proud to be the first and to also experience some backlash from your original family tribe because "that's just not the way we do things back home."

Get a job in the US:

I couldn't have possibly written a book about how to find a job or help my clients do the same if I hadn't experienced what it was like job searching myself.

When I started, I graduated with a (pretty much) worthless degree, having minimal skills, no job experience and a great sense of entitlement.

However, I overcame this by cold e-mailing 100 CEOs, going through numerous interviews, and getting offers.

Help my clients land $100,000+ a year jobs:

You wouldn't be here reading if I hadn't had the experience of helping my clients land 6-figure jobs, and it took me time to land clients and coach them on how to find these jobs.

Helping Family Members Integrate into the US

Throughout these 16 years in the US, I was also able to see my grandmother's immigration experience at age 72, as well as my mother's experience of immigrating to the US at age 33.

I have truly been blessed to be in a unique position to teach immigrants to the US how to successfully find their dream job and create their dream life.

This book is specifically tailored to those who wake up in the middle of the night wondering if they can't get a job because they are immigrants.

This book is for those people who wake up with nightmares about not being able to get their H-

1Bs, OPTs, CPTs, and T-N visas.

It is for those who have wondered whether their classmates, friends, and peers understood their accents.

It is dedicated to the job seeker who wondered if they didn't get that offer because of "cultural reasons."

I hope you will not only be able to implement the job hunting strategies I teach to help you get closer to your dream job but also to live the life that you dreamed of in the US.

End of Chapter Bonus:

Claim your book bonus video "How to Land Any Job You want by clicking here:

http://employedimmigrant.com/bookbonus

CHAPTER 2: HOW TO MAKE IT IN AMERICA

When will you know when you've "made it"?

America has its own version of the American dream, but I believe that you must first understand what "making it" means to you.

Does it mean being a millionaire with your own business?

Does it mean sending all your children to good colleges?

Does it mean doing whatever you want without fear or judgment from those around you?

I can't define it for you because it depends on your own definition. And if you don't know your own definition, you've got some work to do.

I always believe in beginning with the end in mind, and your life in the US will be much better if you have at least a rough idea of where you want to end up.

For me, I wanted to be successful in the sense of being famous, rich, able to do whatever I wanted, and have serious fuck you money (meaning I had the freedom to piss people off if I wanted to because I have a financial safety net to do what I wanted and not have to answer to anyone else)

Obviously, my dream is not everyone else's dreams. My family members have dramatically different dreams than me.

I came to the US at age 10, and my mother came to the US at 33, and my grandmother came at age 72.

You can just imagine how different our expectations are for what success means to ourselves.

For one, it may mean having a stable job. For another, it may be being with family. There is no right or wrong, but it must be right for you.

Inevitably, as an immigrant, you will face opposition to your dreams from people around you, simply because you have different perspectives.

People will disagree with you, but you must learn to hold your own and to fight for your dreams (fyi dreams don't happen by default, you have to work on it)

The funny thing is, there is DEFINITELY a Chinese script for being successful, just as much as there is an American definition of success.

But what's the point if you don't know what the

definition of successful is for yourself?

For some, it may mean getting their dream job in their chosen field. For others, it may mean starting a business. It may mean taking a shitty job to provide for your family. It may also mean taking a pay cut to do what you love.

Or creating your own job where you don't have to compromise anything.

The important thing to take away from this section is to understand your position.

The reason I say this is that when we are younger, we are given a script from our upbringing, but if you are to grow up, no less move to another country or continent, you need to create your own definitions of success.

This is not just a book—this is a *workbook* that I expect you to get results from, so take out a pen and a piece of paper and write down your own answers to these questions to be crystal clear on where you want to be:

1. The definition of success in my home country is:

_____
_____
_____
_____

2. The definition of success in the US is:
_____
_____
_____
_____

3. The definition of success in my family is:
_____
_____
_____
_____

4. My own definition of success is:
_____
_____
_____
_____

5. Where I see myself in a year:
_____
_____
_____
_____

6. Are there any reasons I think I can't get there?
_____
_____
_____
_____

7. What is the reason why I CAN get there?
_____
_____

8. The reason why I came to the US is because:

The Curse of Being Highly Educated & How to Reverse It

I need to talk about this in this chapter because many immigrants who come to the US are the elite in their home countries.

Many are highly educated—I know because my clients have way more degrees than me—with master's degrees, PhDs, MBAs, professional degrees, etc, some with multiple degrees in different fields.

But what is the curse that I'm talking about?

The curse is not only limited to immigrants, but it also manifests especially in education-centered cultures.

And it's this: just because you're highly educated, it doesn't mean that you'll be able to get the job.

This may seem insane to many of us who grew up in cultures where if we do well on a test, historically we are guaranteed a cushy civil servant job for life.

This is not so in the US now.

In the US, you may be the most educated person in the room, and given the benefit of the doubt because of your education, but ultimately, to become an employed immigrant, you absolutely must understand that just because you're educated, it doesn't mean you can get a job.

But you WILL be guaranteed to find a job if you know how to navigate the American job search, which is what I will teach you in this book.

Much of it is about how you PACKAGE yourself, including how you present yourself on paper with resumes and cover letters, and also how you sell yourself on interviews and to people who can potentially refer you, and also absolutely how you network.

So this is a friendly reminder to those of us who have felt dumb because we all of a sudden lost our status in our homelands, that it's okay and normal—as long as you get up and start adapting yourself to the US..

I went from being someone who effortlessly got 90% grades in China, to somebody who came to the US and was held back a grade.

Through a lot of weekends spent studying and the ruthless determination to learn English without an accent, I was able to skip a grade. So understand that this phase is temporary, and with effort, you'll be able to navigate this system with much more ease later.

And a note to those who are considering to get yet ANOTHER degree, think about this:

It's great if you are going to get a degree because you truly love it, but for those who are considering another degree—when you get your degree and graduate, ask yourself— will you get more interviews or will you be in the exact same situation you are in now?

Sometimes more education is paralysis—we are scared of the job market and would rather hide under the name of school than to risk rejection, but guess what—you have to face some amount of rejection to get the job.

So for those who are considering another few years and hundreds of thousands of more debt, ask yourself if you truly want a degree or just don't know how to job hunt (yet). Your answer may save you many years and financial hardships down the line.

From Rejected Busboy to Millionaire: The Immigrant Who Crossed the Border 16 Times

Every time I type out this story, I cry.

And this time is no exception.

This is a story that I want to share with every immigrant who's come up from the bottom.

Back in May, I went to a business conference in Vegas.

I shared my story at the microphone, and the host introduced me to another immigrant, Miguel.

Miguel said something at the stage that struck me deeply:

"If you are not rich in the US, you are either stupid, lazy, or a combination of both."

He then proceeded to tell his story:

Miguel crossed the border 16 times.

Each time he came back to the US.

He was rejected as a busboy at a restaurant, but kept coming back again and again, annoying the hell out of the owner but finally getting the job.

He worked up the chain and bought the restaurant , becoming the owner of the restaurant he used to wash dishes at.

He is now a millionaire who owns ATMs across the country.

I don't think it's an accident that immigrants are 4x as likely as native-born Americans to be millionaires.

Know that where you are right now doesn't matter. All that matters is where you're going.

(I am not an authority on legal/illegal immigration, I am sharing this story to illustrate the point that if you are already in the US, you are in a place that so many people envy and would risk to

For your end of chapter assignment, I want you to write down what you are looking to achieve in the US:

_____
_____
_____

What are you willing to sacrifice?

_____
_____
_____

End of Chapter Bonus:

Want to see how you can land any job you want?

Visit http://www.Employedimmigrant.com/bookbonus to claim your book bonus now!

CHAPTER 3: SUCCEEDING IN THE US FROM AGE 0 TO 100

I didn't fly all the way across the Pacific Ocean to lead a mediocre life.

As immigrants, we always have ties to our homeland, and many times it means bringing over our family, extended family, and entire extended villages.

More likely than not, if you are reading this, you are the first in the family to come to the US.

I created this chapter because it is absolutely important for learning how you can manage your own expectations as well as your family's expectations of being here.

Many of my clients tell me that their parents want them to go back home and there is sadly a lot of conflicts around whether they should stay or go, but one thing I've discovered is that learning to deal with immigration in the US at different ages will be extremely helpful in easing tensions, especially when you are job searching.

Childhood

I came to the US when I was 10 years old, and the most important advice I can give you if you have a child that's just arrived in the US, is to absolutely give that child a chance to learn English and to play with friends who speak English.

When I first came to the US, I went to a Catholic school of 300 students, where there were no ESL programs, and where I was the only immigrant.

It was sink or swim time.

Even though I didn't get it at the time, my mom literally talked the principal, vice principal, and a few other teachers into accepting me without doing any tests that other students were required to do, just on the merit of my drawing and piano skills.

(You've gotta hand it to immigrants who never take no for an answer and a mother who was tired of having to do more immunization tests and thought the best was possible for her daughter!)

So I want to say a thank you to my mother for being an early rule breaker who saw that it was helpful for me to be surrounded by English speakers and to integrate into the US as quickly as possible, even if it meant more pain in the beginning.

I can't teach you how to parent, I will say that in my own experience that while there may be conflicts that arise with your child, the best thing you can do is to keep open communications so that your child understands your decisions.

Teenage Years

This is a pretty tough age to come to the US, as many of my past college application clients I've worked with have had a tough time to deal with during this age.

Many exchange students also come during this time. Having a community around you is EXTREMELY important.

Even though it's a bit harder to assimilate as a teenager, the great thing is that teenagers know better than children, and generally, if they keep up with the culture, they are going to stand a better chance of learning more about their adoptive culture.

Higher Education

You know what's amazing to me about America?

Any time you walk into a college campus, you may see people who are 40, 50, even 80 years old pursuing higher education.

Nobody bats an eye, nobody is singled out for being "weird", because it's accepted that we are all somewhat weird here, especially in college.

College in the US is a mix of everything. You get community colleges where you can knock out 2 years of general education at a budget price, you get state colleges, private institutions, and of course, the Ivies.

There's a saying in China that Chinese universities are difficult to get into and easy to get out of, whereas American universities are easy to get into but difficult to get out of.

I went to an academically rigorous school, so I will advise this: Do not take tons of difficult classes in your first semester in order to "prove" that you're smart.

Make sure you learn the ways of living on your own, getting internships that will help you get jobs (I learned this the hard way), and learning how to manage your relationships.

Even if you started out at a shitty school, you can always transfer, and you can always make something of yourself even if you decide not to pursue higher education.

Working Age

A majority of the people who are reading this book are of working age, and the most important skill you can learn is networking.

Make sure that you make friends with everyone, and I highly suggest you find a friend who can explain the cultural differences in the workplace between your home country and the US.

I've had countless clients commit faux pas that they didn't know.

One of my best clients told me a story about how he gifted perfume to his female boss and got fired—he never had any alternative intentions, because in his country it is very normal, but as you can imagine in the US it could be interpreted differently, so make sure you get a trusted friend to teach you the subtle cultural aspects of the US.

Buy your friend dinner or coffee and get all the information you can about acceptable workplace behavior so that you are prepared for when you do work.

Middle Age

I can't speak from personal experience on this, but what I've seen from my parents' generation is that it may take a tough toll on the ego to be in a new place and to not have your age or seniority revered as much as it was in your old country.

The best thing you can do is not impose your own limitations of what was possible in your old country on what your experiences are in the US.

Just because you are first generation doesn't mean that you have to suffer and be a martyr for everything.

The best thing you can do for yourself is to make sure that you are taking care of yourself and your own mental health during this transition so you can help your family by first helping yourself.

Golden Years

My grandma came to the US when she was 72, and she was the happiest in the US when she was enrolled in the adult school.

I highly encourage any immigrants in their golden years to find a community they can be with, since many of their children are at work and their grandchildren at school, while many older immigrants do not drive and thus are not mobile.

This is the one time where I recommend that you help them by introducing them to people from their culture, as in their advanced age, it is much more difficult and less desirable for them to adapt.

The isolation in the US, due to how far apart many essential places are from each other, can be detrimental to older members, so make sure that you help your older family members adapt by giving them a community they can be a part of in the US.

CHAPTER 4: FINDING THE RIGHT JOB FOR YOU

There are 2 schools of thought on finding the right job for you.

There's the school where you go where you fit the best. There's the other school where you create your own best fit.

Both methods have worked, because I've tried them.

I've been a business analyst in a San Francisco consultancy, I've been a sushi waitress, I've been a bookstore cashier, I've owned my own businesses.

Those I loved and those I didn't, both made money.

The Traditional Route

If you go the first route, it's much easier.

You study what field you want to move into, and you get a job via internships or recommendations from family and friends, and then you move up the ladder.

Many of my clients get jobs that way, as optical engineers are more likely to get jobs as optical engineers, and many software engineers become software engineers after they graduate (easiest job title to find an H-1B visa as well).

Creating Your Own Job

The second route is the route that I personally took.

I firmly believe that your major is not your job.

It's actually the skills that you have plus the network that you develop.

I worked all throughout my 4 years of college in work-study jobs, but never had a real internship and was too spread out to think about what I really wanted to do.

I switched from a grueling architecture degree program to urban studies so I could spend more time studying online marketing while finishing school in time, and after I received my urban studies degree, I took off to backpack Thailand and Malaysia after graduation.

And then—boom!

Back to the reality that I needed to find a job.

I remember sitting on the floor of my Berkeley apartment wondering why the hell I didn't receive a single job offer.

I spent some time feeling sorry about myself but then I realized it wasn't helping me at all.

I also decided that if I didn't have skills, I would make up for it with numbers—I would get as many interview opportunities as possible, no matter how many rejections I would get.

What I did next was hardcore and guerrilla: I invested a lot of energy, time, and money in different programs, books, and hours networking at coffee meetings with people who had the job I wanted.

After sending 100 personalized e-mails to CEOs around the Bay Area, I was finally able to get about 10 interviews.

The job that I finally took had an interesting start: I was browsing LinkedIn, when I found a CEO at an online marketing consultancy in SF. I decided it wouldn't hurt if I sent an e- mail, and I wrote the following:

Dear Boss,

Hi! I saw your site while researching digital marketing agencies around the bay area. My name is Li, and I've had SEO and AdWords experience. I'm curious to hear if you're looking for any interns at the moment.

Let me know if you have any questions, and if you're interested, I can send you my resume.

Thanks!

Li

Simple message that I wasn't sure if I was going to get a response for.

Lo and behold, Wednesday I sent out the message, and in a few hours, I got a request from the boss about my resume, and on Friday I had booked a Skype interview.

Even though I was in Berkeley and the boss was

traveling around the Black Forest in Germany, we did a Skype call, and at the end of it he decided to give me an offer and created the position of a business analyst for me.

I was extremely happy that I finally had finally gotten an offer!

I had to look up in the Haas business library what the hell a business analyst was, and I accepted it after I understood what it involved.

Most importantly, this showed me that even with no experience and a worthless degree, I could get a job.

(Let's face it, I picked that degree was because, well, I had to pick *something* to graduate)

So there are both of the ways of getting a job, but what is absolutely necessary is getting clear on what job you want.

And that's where your coffee networking meetings come in.

This is what I suggest to all my clients: network with people who you think have jobs you'd like.

I've helped one of my star clients transition from being a social media manager to a UX designer through this method.

You absolutely cannot come into the job market saying, "I have this degree; what jobs do you have for me?"

You must be clear on what sort of jobs YOU want.

The days of expecting a higher authority to tell you what to do without extensive research on your part are over.

(Yes, my boss suggested the business analyst job, but I was extremely specific in my e-mail about the skills I had in SEO and online marketing and the companies that I targeted.)

So if an urban studies major can become a business analyst, whatever degree you have, you can get your job.

I've had clients who went from an accounting degree to becoming a tax associate, I've helped PhDs get GIS (geographic information systems) analyst jobs in the government, and I've helped my clients go from manual labor jobs to interviewing at Coca-Cola.

If you can dream it, it is possible for you.

Here is the homework for this section:

What is your dream job title?
_____
_____
_____

What is a job that your friend/family member has that you find interesting?
_____
_____

What is your dream company?

Who can you contact now who is already working in your dream company in the United States?

What would you love to be doing every day in your job?

What would you HATE to be doing every day in your job? (Knowing what you don't want is as important as knowing what you do want.)

What actions do you need to take to reach your dream company right now?

_____
_____
_____

End of Chapter Bonus:

Want to learn my system of how to land your dream job in the US? Join the Employed Immigrant Bootcamp by visiting www.Employedimmigrant.com to accelerate your job search now!

CHAPTER 5: THE ONLY 2 THINGS THAT MATTER ON THE JOB SEARCH

The Only Questions I Ask on Career Assessment Calls

If you apply for a 30-minute career consult at www.FreeCallwithLi.com and if you are accepted, you get a chance to get a career assessment with me. Out of the hundreds of calls I have taken, I do ask about your situation and where you want to be, but I really only ask 2 core questions:

"How many interviews have you had?"

and

"How many job offers do you have?"

These are the only 2 questions that matter.

Because getting a job is actually very SIMPLE.

You just have to get interviews in front of people who have the decision-making power to hire you, and to convince them to hire you.

If you aren't getting enough interviews, it's time to go out and network with people that can either: A) hire you (this is the best, but scariest for job seekers) or B) refer you (these are people who are already working in companies that you'd like to work for).

Why Mass Resume Submission is Dead

Notice that I don't devote a section to resumes, because the Internet has killed mass resume submission.

Now don't get me wrong, I understand how difficult it can be to submit 2,000 resumes and not get a single response.

But it's also incredibly easy to just click a button, just as it is incredibly easy to reject a piece of paper.

What is truly DIFFICULT is building relationships. It's also difficult to turn down somebody when they are referred.

And here's why mass resume submission doesn't work:

Think about the last time you sold furniture on Craigslist. At least for me, within 30 minutes of posting the chair, I had 20 e-mail responses asking me when they could pick it up.

Now imagine this for the job search.

Hell, you can just LOOK at LinkedIn job posts, and you'll see 200 people competing for a very entry level job.

You could be the best of the best and be the 189th person before the boss throws up her hands and says "I'm tired of interviewing after 8 people!" and your efforts are ashes to dust—gone.

No doubt you COULD submit resumes and get a job that way, but just bear in mind this method has been destroyed by the Internet (anyone with an Internet connection in the world could be your competition), and bear in mind that 80% of jobs in the US are filled via referral.

I can hear your eyes rolling through the screen, but the truth is that if the rules are that people hire people they know first, instead of hating networking, why not learn the rules and win the game?

What if I am Not Good Enough Yet?

Ah, you have hit one of my pet peeves: the EASIEST way to piss me off is to say you want something and then have an excuse as to why you can't get it.

YES, thinking that you're not good enough IS an excuse.

Think about this: Are you the person who decides whether or not you are hired?

HELL NO!

It's the boss that decides whether or not you are good enough!

But what is YOUR job when it comes to the job search?

Your duty is to get yourself out there, let your family and friends and everyone you meet to know that you are available for hire.

Let the odds be in your favor by putting yourself out there, so that when there is a vacancy, you are the first person they think of.

Yes, networking can be a short-term game, but generally, you want to be able to build it before you need it.

You know what the US idolizes?

Young college drop outs who start a billion dollar company from their parents' garage with zero qualifications.

Rebels who break away from their motherland (the original Brexit) and have the guts to establish a new country.

Saying that they're the #1 country in the world, over and over again.

So understand that you are in a country that absolutely rewards risk takers—what's the worst that can happen to your job search?

Nothing.

Literally, the worst that can happen is that nothing happens, so why not take the risk of telling people you're looking for a job?

CHAPTER 6: CREATING A NETWORK FROM NOTHING

Stop Hanging Out with Your "People"

One of the biggest problems I hear while working with my clients is that they always say **they don't know anyone**.

And the people who they know?

They say they can't help them with the job search.

I completely understand this.

When you first come to a foreign country, when you hear somebody speaking your hometown dialect, your eyes well up with tears.

When you smell that dish you took for granted, you scarf it down because it reminds you of home so much.

But when it comes to the job search, it's time to stop hanging out with "your people".

I'm not saying you should abandon all your friends and never go to eat hotpot with your homies or karaoke on the weekend.

What I am saying is to DIVERSIFY your network.

It can be people from your country as well, but you HAVE to hang out with people who have the job that you want.

One of the quotes from the Olsen twins is gold, and it's no wonder that they are great entrepreneurs: **"Only take advice from people you'd like to trade places with."**

If you are always hanging out with people who want to go back to their home country, how do you expect to find a job with a network like that?

You need to stop hanging out with people who have all given up on the H-1B search and gone home when YOU want to stay in the US. (I'm just making a wild assumption since you're reading this book, but hey, I may be wrong.)

The Meetings That Will Change Your Career

Coffee meetings are one of my favorite and most strategic things that I teach my clients.

When done right, they will give you a huge advantage over other job seekers who do not have an "in" like you do, and they can save you from wasting a ton of time working in a position that is not for you, all in just one conversation.

I was able to learn a ton about a company after a coffee meeting.

I remember watching an interview about an SEO company that fascinated me and wondering if I could get in touch with one of the employees there.

I used LinkedIn.com to look up someone who worked there, and lo and behold, found an employee who lived in my city.

I crafted an e-mail talking about how I heard about the company and was interested in his website on conversion rate optimization, and I asked if we could meet at a Berkeley cafe (my treat) to discuss what it was like working there.

When we met at the cafe, he told me so much behind-the-scenes advice that would not have been possible to find out just via Googling.

In the end, I knew so much about his company, and

he even offered a referral for me, and the CEO responded in about 20 minutes.

This definitely would not have been possible had it not been for his referral.

As you can see, even if you know nobody and have nothing, you can still reach out to people who can refer you, and this may be the way you land your dream job.

I give you the exact template on how to network to turn strangers into professional contacts on LinkedIn and via e-mail at my Employed Immigrant Bootcamp here: www.employedimmigrant.com

How to Commit Career Suicide

You may think it's strange that I put this section here, but I would be remiss if I did not include this story.

I've given talks at the University of California at Irvine's Chinese Student Association, where some students raised their hand and asked, "Is this type of networking like harassment?"

I don't think networking is harassment if it's done right.

But there is a WRONG way to do it.

I want all of the readers of my book to leave with an understanding of what it means to be a true networker and not just a user.

Here's how NOT to do networking:

4 years ago, I went through one of the career training courses that warned against being the type of person who asks people for help and never gives back.

I never thought it would be a concern for me until I experienced this myself. A few years ago I referred somebody from my school to a startup.

She was very responsive when I was going to help her, and I never heard back from her again until about a week ago when she requested a career breakthrough call with me.

Guess what?

In her e-mail, she wrote that **she got the internship 3 years ago through me.**

And I never heard back from her again until she needed my help again.

I forgot about this until she recently e-mailed me about her wanting to get a job, and in that, she said she was able to get the startup internship via my referral.

"Wow!" I thought. I was doing career coaching 3 years before I actually started my business!

And also I was thinking . . .

What the fuck? You got a job through me, and you never told me?

I did give her another chance on the call and helped her as much as I could during the breakthrough call.

At the end, I decided to ask her if she got the job years ago, and her response was **"Oh, it wasn't a job; it was just an internship."**

No mention of thank you, gratitude, appreciation, zilch.

If you are reading this message, make sure that you never become someone like her.

Don't be the person who reaches out when you need somebody else's help, never say thank you when they help you do something, and yet still have the balls to ask for help again from the same person.

I have removed her from my connections, and I will never help her again.

Let this be a warning to you so you can become not only someone who is able to help themselves but someone who always acknowledges help when they receive it.

I hope you use what I learned, to become a true networker—somebody who says thank you when they are given help and somebody who looks for ways to help others, not just somebody who gives networking a bad name and just uses others.

Make sure to pay the gift of networking forward by referring other qualified candidates who reach out to you as well.

End of Book Bonus: Want to learn the ins and outs of networking? Visit www.EmployedImmigrant.com.

CHAPTER 7: ACING JOB INTERVIEWS LIKE A ROCKSTAR

I absolutely love coaching my clients on interviews, because it's about something I love--storytelling.

As much as you may think it's about the qualifications and being "the best man/woman" who wins, it's as much about the package as it is about the substance.

Think about this: if you've managed to make it to the interview round, that means that they have at least skimmed your resume and thought that you were at least qualified minimally for them to spend an hour to talk to you.

The interview is NOT just about your technical qualifications; **it's mostly about how you fit and if you can do the job at the company.**

So if you regurgitate your resume thinking that's how you're going to win at the interview, that's why you don't have a job yet.

I truly believe that storytelling is the key to acing a good job interview, and you don't even have to be good at English to tell good stories. You do need a structure, and you do need practice, but those are all skills that you can learn and develop.

The funny thing is I've talked to foreign PhDs who have lamented about how they envy American job seekers who can just joke around the office.

But guess what? It's not the jokes that got them in; **it's the fact that they created rapport.**

Rather than becoming a jokester, it's better to learn how to tell stories that reflect your professional competence.

This is why you'll see people with heavy accents running Silicon Valley, and how half of all PhDs being from a foreign country.

It's not about perfect English, but how you express yourself.

Why Should I Hire You?

People are always shocked when I ask this question on mock interviews, but the truth is, even if the interviewer doesn't ask you explicitly, they are thinking it, 100% of the time.

This question is actually the core of the interview.

If you don't know how to answer this question on the interview, you might as well not go at all.

When you say, "I'm passionate about the job," my face goes blank.

So what?

Anybody else who applies for the job can say the same thing.

You talk ad infinitum about your education, but what makes you different from any classmate of yours who graduated from the same school?

You have 3 years of experience? The other person has 5. Are you dead in the water yet? To simplify the job search, the only thing that you should make an appeal to is 2 things:

1. How you can help the company make money.
2. How you can help the company save time.

Obviously, my clients with finance backgrounds because it's very easy to compare numbers to numbers and how much money you've helped a company make.

And also, especially for my H-1B seeking friends--the company will be paying an extra $7,000 for you just to file your paperwork, will you make it worthwhile for them?

In this case, it is more important than ever for you to say what you're worth.

So what does this mean? Just saying that you know how to read financial statements is not enough. Just saying that you know different programming languages doesn't cut it.

Here are some examples of extremely short but effective stories that my clients have told on job interviews:

"I have helped companies grow from $20,000 in revenue to $2 million." "I was able to help create an Excel app that saved 360 hours of data entry time." "I was able to help 10 people save $5,000 while working as a VITA IRS volunteer."

Do you see how short these stories are but how impactful they can be to a company?

Bottom line is that a company wants to hire people who can grow them or help them save time, and if you know how to tell stories from this angle, you've got it halfway made already.

Storytellers Shall Inherit the Earth

Have you heard of the quote from the Bible,"The meek shall inherit the earth?"

I call bullshit.

Everywhere I look, the storytellers rule the earth.

For most of the past 2000+ years of civilization, religion has been running the world.

Is it weird that we still follow it based on the books in a story?

Similarly, we follow stories all our lives, whether you follow Buddha, Jesus, Mohammad, Ahura Mazda, Abraham, or your whoever your denomination is, they all had stories, and they rallied their followers with their stories.

We've never met them in person, but we have internalized their stories into our own cultures and identities.

This is what you need to do with your interviews as well. Here's why: **HOW you describe yourself is incredibly important.**

It can mean the difference between someone who becomes wildly in love with you v. someone who finds you absolutely repulsive.

A few months ago I got so good at what I did that I saw my work as almost boring and routine.

Thankfully, I snapped out of this and realized what I REALLY do. I create the next Buddha and the next Jesus.

Allow me to explain: Most of the clients who come to me are incredibly smart. They are the crème de la crème in their home countries.

They have PhDs and master's degrees and have owned businesses in their countries, but the ONLY thing that's separating them between their dream jobs and their current position is ONE thing.

HOW they tell their stories.

They say that the world was dominated by religion for the past 2,000 years, and I would agree. As a former Catholic school student, I know how much Christianity influenced the laws, customs, and business practices of Western society.

So even though Buddha and Jesus are long gone, what remains are their stories.

We can visually see a starving Buddha trying to see the opposite of his royal, princely childhood.

We can see Jesus's parables that were taught to his disciples and relate them to our daily lives.

(Being read begrudgingly by 14 year old schoolchildren in religion class in Catholic school, but read nonetheless.)

Don't you think that it's INSANE that even after thousands of years we are still reading their stories?

And guess what, I am doing the same for my clients by teaching them to immortalize themselves in story, whereas before they would be rejected 15 times by interviewers. Now one of my longest-term clients has successfully gotten 2 jobs, and each time the job was better.

I help them craft the stories, and then the stories live on through word of mouth and are immortalized on paper as their cover letters and their resumes, and hopefully eventually they'll be telling their story at the next company.

Because storytelling is all that an interview is.

You may not be able to directly tell who's better than who from the resume, but think about anyone you remember; you have a story about them.

You have a story about why you deserve the job.

You have a story about why you don't deserve the job.

You have a story about why being wealthy is what you want.

Or a story about how rich people are worse people.

You have a story about how you fell in love.

And how you fell out of love.

And I am lucky enough to be able to share this skill with the coolest, craziest, most adventurous people who decided to say fuck it to their old life and create a brand new dream.

So periodically I have to slap myself for being ungrateful for what I do, because what I GET to do is create COMPANY LEGENDS that live on, even when they move to different jobs.

What I get to CO-CREATE is an amazing dream destiny for people who I was chosen to work with.

Am I being sacrilegious for saying they may be gods?

Maybe a little, but YOU are as much of a LEGEND in your own mind as you allow yourself to be.

It is a privilege to have been able to work with my clients and a privilege to be able to shape their new stories in a new land, so they can be paid and valued in the companies they love.

And I won't be forgetting what I truly do anytime soon: telling the best stories so that my clients' dreams can live on.

Can't Take a Hit, Can't Be a Champ

At this point, I have to talk about something that inevitably comes up on the job search: rejection.

If you don't know how to handle failure, you can't handle success.

Why?

There are tons of jobs out there, but **you have to manage your emotions when it comes to job searching** because not every company wants you, nor do you want to work for any company (this book is aimed at 6-figure job seekers, after all).

Instead of viewing the rejection as personal, understand that getting a rejection e-mail

gives you the advantage of being able to ask them WHY they rejected you.

This feedback is not only going to be helpful for your job search now but for every other company you interview with in the future.

Weeping over 1 company rejection for a week is not only detrimental for taking action for your job search but also bad for your mental health.

It's nothing personal, just that you're not a good fit to work there. The universe is preparing something equal or even better for you.

My rule is that it's okay to cry for 2 minutes over

something, and after that, move on with your life.

I was rejected 90 times during my first job search.

Had I felt sorry for myself and not applied 10 more times, I would not have gotten 10 interviews.

I'm not saying that once you apply for 90, you'll get the job, but it is the spirit of not giving a fuck how many people said you weren't good enough and keeping going regardless of what it looks like NOW, but keeping going because you know there's a better future waiting for you, if only you'll keep going.

The job search can be an emotional roller coaster. You are the one managing it, so make sure that you're not steering yourself wrong.

Remember: you're a champ, you can take a hit!

CHAPTER 8: HOW TO MAKE $100,000+ A YEAR

This is the chapter you've been waiting for, and there are 2 elements to landing a $100,000+ a year job:

1. The job title

2. How well you negotiate

That's it. Very simple, so the first thing you want to research is which jobs are in that $100,000 range.

There are tons of 6-figure jobs, and here are some of them:

1. Software developers (median salary: $102,880)

2. Sales managers (median salary: $110,660)

3. Financial managers (median salary: $115,320)

4. Pharmacists (median salary: $120,950)

5. Lawyers (median salary: $114,970)

6. Human resource managers (median salary: $102,780)

7. Marketing managers (median salary: $127,130)

8. Computer & information system managers (median salary: $127,640)

9. Architectural & engineering managers (median salary: $130,620)

10. Chief executives (median salary: $173,320)
11. Family & General Practitioners (median salary: $180,180)

(Source: http://247wallst.com/special-report/2015/09/08/the-jobs-paying-americans-the- most/4/.)

Not to make you think that only these jobs can make 6 figures, according to Forbes, here are some 22 surprising jobs that also can make it to the 6-figure job category:

1. Makeup artists

2. Technical writers

3. Gaming managers

4. Post-secondary home economics teachers

5. Captains of water vessels

6. Art directors

7. Transportation inspectors

8. Broadcast news analysts

9. Farmers, ranchers & agricultural managers

10. Insurance sales agents

11. Education administrators

12. Writers & authors

13. Film & video editors

14. Arbitrators & mediators

15. Multimedia artists & animators

16. Elevator installers & repairers

17. Loan officers

18. Postsecondary art, drama & music teachers

19. Database administrator

Via http://www.forbes.com/pictures/efkk45jfek/makeup-artists-theatrical-and- performance-5/#1d87e9b52e36.

As you can see, good paying jobs are not just the conventional types, but there are many jobs where you can MAKE them earn 6 figures.

Whichever job you do decide to pursue, however, I absolutely urge you to learn the skill of salary negotiation because that's what's going to ultimately help you bump up in pay grades and get you the paycheck that YOU want.

The Vegas Hotel Text Coaching Session That Landed My Client a $115,000 Job

One of the proudest moments of my career happened in a Las Vegas hotel.

I was there for a business conference, and during the break, I got a text from my client. She was offered a job, and she was very nervous about how to negotiate the salary.

I shared with her the steps of how to job search and a module from the Employed Immigrant Bootcamp, and after a few hours, she sent me the good news, and here's the WeChat message translated from Chinese to English:

"This afternoon they called me offering a $115,000 base salary, RSUs: $45 K, Annual bonus: 10 percent, Sign on $20 K."

She was happy with what she negotiated and accepted her 6 figure job.

These are the types of texts I get, and I absolutely freaking love them because not only was I able to help my clients, but they have become six-figure earners as well, and it's not just the money but the confidence and ability to do it over and over again.

So understand that a little bit of negotiation can take you a long way in terms of getting the job you want.

If you are interested in checking out the salary

negotiation module that helped my client land a $115,000 a year job, visit www.EmployedImmigrant.com.

What Street Stall Hawkers Can Do Better Than You

If you travel to China, if you are not a native of the city, it is guaranteed that the street stall hawkers will massively raise their prices.

If you don't know the dialect, maybe a 20% increase, and I've heard street hawkers overcharge white foreigners by 500%.

Not saying it's fair, but, hey, that's just how they make money. And yet, when I talk to Chinese professionals to negotiate, many of them immediately

become scared—**until they actually get the salary they want, like my clients. Put down your perceptions that you must be GIVEN permission to ask for what**

you want.

You have to create your chances of negotiating your salary.

I remember one of my long-term clients who was offered a $50 K job as a developer, which was not very much at all since he had 7.5 years of experience, and we talked about what he truly wanted.

I coached him on the range that he should expect to be looking for as somebody with his experience, and in a week, he was able to land a $75,000 base salary with a $2,000 relocation fee as well as a chance to negotiate in 3 months.

You can negotiate in any position you are in.

The first time I wanted to negotiate as a business analyst, I was turned down, but I kept asking, and after a month, I was able to negotiate a $1,000 raise.

What's the significance of that?

Even if you feel you don't have much to gain, think about how much you might stand to lose.

Consider this:

I've noticed a disturbing trend among recent grads who say "Experience is more important to me than money. I'm willing to work for cheap."

Hold that thought and consider what you may be missing:

If you negotiated a $500 one-time raise, over the course of 40 years invested, you would have $1,398,905.20!

Think about every time you've told yourself "This is too expensive" when you truly wanted to buy something.

Do you want to live this way forever?

Or are you willing to sacrifice 1 hour of your life having an uncomfortable conversation that can add THOUSANDS, if not more, to your monthly paycheck, by just learning ONE thing—negotiation?

I understand it's beyond the comfort zone of most people, and many of my clients have felt the same, UNTIL they negotiated that $115,000 a year base salary with $10,000 signing bonus. They are now all HUGE fans of negotiation.

Why? Because they know how to do it, but most importantly they DID IT. It's much easier when you just push yourself and set a date for it.

When I was first offered a business analyst job, I pushed to negotiate, was denied, but one month later, I scheduled a Friday afternoon salary negotiation appointment with my boss and got a $1,000 raise.

What could a $1,000 extra in your bank account do for you?

ESPECIALLY if you are a woman, you have a unique opportunity to PERSONALLY close the wage gap by negotiating.

Even if it's just to finally get that designer bag you've been eyeing, you can do that if you learn the skill of negotiation.

And let me tell you—ladies, if you want confidence? Learn how to make a fuck ton of money.

That money can buy you anything you want, month after month: you can donate it to charity, take that trip abroad, expand your circle to higher earning friends, and more!

Negotiation enables you to make thousands within just 1 hour (or less).

If you are interested learning salary negotiation, check out www.EmployedImmigrant.com.

You Are Not a Beggar, So Don't Act Like One

If you remember nothing, I want to end this chapter on this note: no matter what, you are not a beggar. You may feel that you can't command this value, but if somebody else was doing the same job as you, you'd probably feel they were more valuable than you.

Stop letting somebody else's value dictate your own value.

If you want a 6-figure life, you've gotta stop sitting down and letting life happen to you. You've gotta make sure that **you're armed with the skills of negotiation.**

There is a right way and wrong way to do this: the wrong way is to wing it, but still, even if you just ask for a negotiation, you increase your chances of getting it.

I absolutely want you to negotiate because if you're underpaid, not only will you have to take a second job, drain your energy, and spend less time with your friends and family, but eventually, you'll also start to resent your job, which is never a good energy to have.

So for the sake of your own self-worth and also the good of the company, negotiate! Companies value negotiation skills in their employees, and if you in any capacity work with other vendors, they'll know that your negotiation skills will help the company save money, and in that case, paying YOU to save the company boatloads more money is infinitely worth it.

Negotiation isn't just limited to money; you can negotiate working on Fridays at home or having flex time; you can negotiate your hours, have the company compensate you for higher education, and more.

When you see highly educated people take jobs that require half their education, when you see people who should be paid more taking multiple jobs, it's not because they're not good enough. It's because they failed at successfully negotiating their worth with their employer.

Remember this next time you meet a foreign PhD driving Ubers: It's really not the objective degrees that help you get a job. It's the amount of effort you put into demanding your worth.

PS: No hate to foreign PhDs who drive Ubers, but one of the biggest pet peeves in my life is seeing people who are highly qualified in one country have all their self-esteem destroyed when they move to a new country.

I'm saying out of love that you CAN do and SHOULD do better and be paid what you are WORTH!

CHAPTER 9: JOB TALES FROM AROUND THE WORLD

This is one of my favorite chapters because it's all about my immigrant friends' experiences in the US.

There was no way I would have covered all the ground just with my own story, and I'm so happy to be able to share with you stories from professionals hailing from Ecuador, Nigeria, Spain, Cameroon, India, China, the US, Indonesia, and more.

If you have your own story, I'd love to hear from you! Please email me at Li@Li-Lin.Net so I can share your success with my community!

Prestigious Jobs, with Ivana Kusijanovic

My name is Ivanna Kusijanovic, and I am originally from Ecuador.

I am currently a life and business coach, working with women entrepreneurs who want to start a location-independent life and business.

I have been in and out of the US several times, the first time when I was 7 and did elementary school here in Boston.

Next I came for 1 year of college when I was 20 and the last time I came (to stay!) was 5 years ago, when I was 27.

I am also a mom of 2 beautiful girls, they are 10 and 5.

What is your background in your home country?

I studied in a private university in Guayaquil, Ecuador, and majored in international relations.

I also studied languages, which is one of my passions. I speak 5 (English, Spanish, Italian, Portuguese, and French).

My initial goal was to be a diplomat, but that was just to have an excuse to travel, until I discovered other things that interest me more and still allow me to travel!

What was your job-hunting experience in the US

like?

Before I get into how I got the type of job that I got here in the states, I do need to mention a brief work history prior to the US, since that inspired me to look for other things to do once I got here.

As mentioned above, my passion was to learn new languages, travel, and live in other countries, etc.

So that's what I did. I set out to live in Italy at first and then in Spain.

I didn't really care what I was doing as long as I got the experience of living and working in several countries.

I found that in Spain, people that worked in the financial industry earned more than others.

They were very respected, and it was considered a very prestigious industry/line of work to be in, so I started working with British expats in Spain, for a British bank.

Without getting into more detail there, fast forward 5 years and I moved to the US. I knew it was relatively easy to find work in the US in the banking world, so I wasn't worried. It's what I knew how to do.

So there I was, 27 years old, looking for a job, and I landed a job in 2 weeks at Wells Fargo!

I was happy as hell, until I got there.

I was the oldest one there by at least 7 years. It was

all hip, fresh outta high school kids, who were doing their first job ever!

I lasted there a few years, and I enjoyed it but found that the industry wasn't as prestigious as I was used to.

I was used to saying "I work in a bank," and it was like saying "I'm the Queen Mother."

In the US, not so much.

That kinda took a toll on my self-esteem.

I saw that people my age were leaving the job, starting their own businesses, buying rental properties, or flipping houses, etc., and I was lost.

I thought that was my career, my life, and that I had found a company in which I could be a "lifer" but happy about it, not in the bad sense.

Also, in other countries, I was used to having a "permanent contract" be synonymous with success as well. Again, in the US, not so much; a permanent contract doesn't really mean much at all.

When I hit 30... I really started to hear the conversations like, "What is she still doing here?"

"Would you want to still be here when you're 30?"

Ugh, that killed me!

But I used it for good and started researching other options.

I was happy with my job—don't get me wrong—I just out grew it. It also coincided with the fact that I got divorced, and my ex-husband and I shared finances.

He would have never been onboard with me investing in starting a business of my own.

This is also something I took to my advantage when I did become financially independent from him.

After several months of heavy research about ways to find other sources of income and means of independence, I came to blogging and coaching online/over the phone.

I fell in love with the idea and started a coaching business.

I have been in business now for a little over a year and am currently working on getting certified as a business coach!

If you could only give one piece of advice, what would you say to new immigrants to the US about the job search?

What's considered cool/elegant/prestigious in one country, isn't, necessarily, in another.

Also, If you come from a country in which public pensions, socialized medicine, education, paid time off, and paid maternity leaves are a given, you better do your research here.

When you interview in other countries, you really want the job, and you really make yourself humble in the situation.

Here, you also need to interview your potential employer; be confident and ask about your benefits, time off, potential maternity leaves, sick days, etc. You need the job, but remember, they need good workers too.

How can we connect with you?

You can find out more about me at www.queenlifebydesign.com and also connect with me on Facebook at Ivanna Kusijanovic!

How to Have an Accent & Still Find a Kickass Job, with Margaret Olatunbosun

I was born and raised in Lagos, Nigeria, in the late 1980s in a middle-class family.

Unlike my American colleagues, we chose our career paths as early as the 8th grade. I was convinced that I'd be a journalist, so nobody was surprised when I selected mass communication & journalism as my major right out of high school.

Well, two semesters into my program, my father had good news for us: we could finally travel to America and be reunited.

My arrival to the USA in 2007 was the beginning of my career and identity confusion.

But my confusion was nothing compared to the mess waiting for me as a new graduate. Armed with degrees in health services administration and gerontology, a minor in management, and 3 completed internships, I wanted to be a nursing home administrator.

So I picked up the phone and dialed the numbers to several healthcare facilities. I asked for internship opportunities, and continuously flaunted my high GPA and summa cum laude.

But the responses were cold. I remember crying after a particular encounter because the manager made fun of my accent and asked me to learn how to communicate before anything.

Realizing that my degrees weren't going to help me, I thought about my part-time gigs throughout college.

During my senior year, I was the clinical systems support personnel for a huge healthcare facility and learned about healthcare informatics in the process.

So I began to connect and build relationships with individuals in clinical systems management.

By doing this, I was able to get jobs that were not advertised and was able to take a rest on sending out job applications.

Here's my advice to new immigrants: **Forget about job titles and how much money you want to make annually.**

Instead, do this: imagine your dream lifestyle for the next 5 years, 10 years, and 20 years.

Then make career decisions that will support you as you make your transitions.

Why?

Even if you want to make $67,000 per year in the next 5 years, if your dream lifestyle cannot be supported, you will find yourself constantly feeling frustrated.

For me, this dream lifestyle means the ability to work from anywhere while getting paid.

As a copywriter, I help brilliant but frustrated

online entrepreneurs get seen, get hired, and get paid for their skills.

I do this by helping them create irresistible offers and crafting compelling copy that describes what they sell so they can profit from their brilliance.

And here's the best part: I can serve my clients in and out of the hospital if I want. You also don't have to choose one or the other.

Two seemingly unrelated passions can coexist, and I am living proof of that.

If you want to learn more about what I do and how I serve my clients, you can find me at: www.margaretolat.com, and Facebook: www.facebook.com/margaretolat7

Helping Thousands Find Their Jobs via Albert's List, with Albert Qian

My name is Albert Qian. I was born and raised in Silicon Valley, and am now living in Orange County working as a marketing manager for a technology consulting firm.

I started out my career with an information systems degree and worked in social media for several years before moving into more strategic marketing roles.

I was born in the United States about 7 years after my parents immigrated here from China. I didn't really discover this or appreciate the situation until later, but my parents definitely did a great job of winging it while raising me.

They both had no idea what it meant to grow up in the United States, so things like prom, field trips, and book reports were very new.

My parents were both engineers and worked in engineering in Silicon Valley for 30 years before their retirement in 2015.

When I made the decision to go into marketing, they had no way of helping me because they had worked and networked within their own silo of careers for the past three decades.

Initially, I had a very fragmented job-hunting experience because I didn't know what I wanted and had no idea where to go for anything.

My process of being able to find jobs was something I learned through a lot of trial and error, and my skill of networking only developed after college—and only after I had gone to my university's LinkedIn page to ask for help.

These days, I often think of what it means to be the child of an immigrant. When my dad landed at San Francisco International Airport in 1980, he had less than $50 to his name and a one-way trip to see my grand uncle.

As an employee in Silicon Valley in the '80s, he made far less than I did at my first job, and lived in an apartment in Campbell.

I am sure he had his doubts, and so did my mother, and as a first-generation child, even though I have my struggles, what really hits home is thinking that my parents didn't immigrate here so that I could half-ass my future.

They immigrated here and raised kids here presumably so their children could be great and make the most of what is offered to them.

As an immigrant, that should be your thought too.

You've worked so hard to get the H1-B, come over here for an education, and make things work.

You have nothing to lose and everything to gain.

Albert runs an amazing community of 16,000+ (and growing) called Albert's List, my clients have found jobs through his group, and you can join here:

http://www.albertslist.org/.

From Spain to Silicon Valley, with Esther Howard

My name is Esther Howard. I am originally from Barcelona (Spain).

I am a software engineer now, but it took me almost a year to learn how the job market works in the US and how important connections are, to find my first job in the Bay Area.

What is your background in your home country?

I was a software engineer back home too. I landed an internship while at school, and that became a full-time job after I graduated.

In order to graduate from my university, you have to do an internship which gives you the experience you need to find a job.

I was lucky to have that; otherwise, my search in the US would've been way harder.

What was your job hunting experience in the US like?

My job hunting in the US was a really hard and long process. Things here are done differently, and I had to learn that the hard way.

Also, I am a very introverted person, so going to meetups and networking events was a very exhausting experience for me.

Besides all this, I had never worked with recruiters before.

If you are lucky enough to find a good recruiter, that person will help you find an amazing job.

But most of the recruiters I worked with would never answer my calls or e-mails after interviews; most of them I never heard from again.

Job hunting is a rough experience, especially in the Bay Area.

If you could only give one piece of advice, what would you say to new immigrants to the US about the job search?

Start making connections! Go to meetups, search for expert advice that can help you in the transition to the US market.

Get to know good recruiters that will truly help you find your perfect position.

How can we connect with you?

My LinkedIn profile is https://www.linkedin.com/in/howardesther13.

From 5-Year-Old English Teacher to TOEFL Master, with Ankita

Hi! I am Ankita, a managing consultant and an entrepreneur.

I coach the Test of English as a Foreign Language ("TOEFL") to non-native English speakers who want to achieve a score of 80 or above on the TOEFL exam.

I am originally from India and now call Washington DC my home. My journey in the United States has been a true "learning" experience.

What is your background in your home country?

I came to the US after finishing my undergraduate degree in accounting. I was a top performer in my university, with a 3.95 GPA.

I received my master's degree in finance from John Hopkins University. I always had a passion for teaching, which led to starting my own coaching business.

As my mother shares, I was only five years old when she found me teaching English vocabulary to fellow children in our neighborhood.

What was your job hunting experience in the US like?

When I first came to the US, I had nobody to guide me through the process of finding a job.

I did my own research without knowing the direction I was heading toward. It was extremely difficult.

I had no network, no interview experience, and worse, nobody to guide me through the day-to-day challenges that all recent immigrants face.

We underestimate how a little mentorship or coaching goes a long way.

If you could only give one piece of advice, what would you tell to new immigrants to the US about the job search?

I believe a lot of things play a role in landing the job you want.

Good networking skills, interview preparation, negotiation, and confidence—all of these things play an extremely important role.

My advice to a job seeker is to attend meetup groups and events, talk to people, find mentors, be confident, and once you have the job offer, NEGOTIATE!

How can we connect with you?

When I look back, I owe my success to my hard work and my decision to go for a master's degree in the US.

This isn't always easy, as they ask for your TOEFL score, and English isn't your first language. That's where I can help you.

I understand your mindset, being an immigrant myself.

I transform that mindset of apprehension into confidence by helping you build your English skills for the TOEFL exam.

With my proven strategies, you can ace all of the sections of the exam and achieve the score you need and want.

Visit my website at www.TOEFLwithAnkita.com for Free TOEFL Tips and to connect with me!

You can also connect with me through my Facebook page:

https://www.facebook.com/TOEFLwithAnkita/

Negotiating Your Teacher's Salary, with Queenie Johnson

As a middle school teacher working in progressive paradigms, I learned the power of making powerful requests to enhance my communication skills.

I used what I had learned from nonviolent communication to declare my value and negotiate a $15 K increase in my pay.

I pushed this newfound skill set a step forward and used it to start MamaBeBrilliant, a personal brand and leadership development company for mompreneurs.

Now I'm teaching entrepreneurs how to communicate their value as the "go-to authority" and accelerate their audience's need for their services.

What is your background?

Born in Jacksonville, Florida, and raised in San Diego, California. I learned early on that I couldn't ask for more money as a teacher.

Taking an unconventional route in my career led me to this funky and creative school on the west side called Pacifica Community Charter.

It's there where I honed my skills, learning to value my voice and opinion and ask for what I want.

What was your job-hunting experience in the US like?

I graduated with a $120,000 degree only to find that we were in an economic downturn.

I wanted to teach, but a law had been signed that schools would no longer hire teachers unless they were "highly-qualified."

This required me to go back to school for another year to get a credential which cost me another $30,000.

In the meantime, I couldn't find a job paying more than $10–12 an hour. Sigh! Eventually, I applied to a few dozen jobs.

I was called for a teaching position that allowed me to serve as the resource teacher for a non-public school.

I was hired to make $13.50 an hour. In my second year on the job, I asked for a raise.

The principle said, "No, we don't have money in the budget." I walked away unfazed by his response.

Instead, I went home and typed up a letter to communicate the value I bring to the school and how my skillset needed to be recognized.

After handing in that letter, a few days later, I received notice that I, in fact, would be getting a raise.

I made $17.50 per hour the next year.

Many people give up when they hear no.

When someone tells me no, it just means they don't

understand what I'm really saying. It just enforces that I need to articulate my value better.

After this, I never took no for an answer.

I asked for two more raises in my career, each yielding a $15–20 K raise.

Teaching is the least respected profession in America.

If I can ask for a raise, you can as an immigrant.

Especially after I found out my colleague was making more than me—$15,000 more than me. EEK. What did I do? I asserted my value and asked for more money.

If you could only give one piece of advice, what would you tell new immigrants to the US about the job search?

Remember that you are bringing value to the company. The company isn't "hiring" you.

You are using your talents to bring a result to the company, and they are giving you cash for that result.

When you recognize this, you show up to the negotiating table with your power. When you recognize your power, you have control.

I'm not simply referring to controlling the situation—but controlling your destiny. Establish what you desire to be paid. Add another $15 K to that price. Remember, no one will be willing to offer you what you're truly worth.

Ask for it.

Be clear. Be unwavering in you quest.

Be certain. Certainty wins all the time.

How can we connect with you?

You can connect with me online here: @MrsQueenieJohnson on Instagram or @MrsQueenieJ on Periscope /Twitter.

Helping H-1B Job Seekers via Technology, with Peng Z

I am originally from China.

I got my BS and MS degrees in China, and then I came to the USA for a doctoral program at West Virginia University.

After 4 years of study, I successfully graduated with a PhD degree in mining engineering.

Then I found a job as a software engineer at a company located in Boston, MA.

After 2 years of work, I decided to move to a warm place; then I hit Clearwater, Florida, which is a big city with nice weather.

The Clearwater Beach is the top beach in the US, and I really like it.

What is your background in your home country?

I was born in Pingdingshan, Henan, China, which is a small town powered by the coal industry.

It is also the reason why I choose mining engineering as my major.

My college life was spent in Henan Polytechnic University, which is located in Jiaozuo, Henan.

I got my BS and MS degrees of mining engineering from this university.

What was your job-hunting experience in the US like?

It is really hard for international students to find their first job in the US, especially for me and my major.

Why? Because there are only around 10 universities that have this major across the entire US. What is worse? When I graduated in 2014, the mining industry was going down all around the world.

All of the mining companies in the US were laying off, and lots of them even went bankrupt.

However, I learned coding by myself when I was in college.

For my first job, there were 20+ candidates, and only I had not majored in computer science.

However, during the coding test, I was the best among them, and even the best in the company's entire recruiting history.

They were surprised and gave me the job offer. To be honest, I was surprised as well.

If you could only give one piece of advice, what would you tell to new immigrants to the US about the job search?

I looked back on my job hunting history and that of others, and I found that job hunting should be carefully planned.

I did not do it well, but you should learn a lesson from

me.

Do not choose those unpopular majors which are not in demand in the job market.

It would be great if you could do some homework to find out those opportunities that are in highly demanded in the US job market.

Job hunting is all about filling the job market's needs.

You need to know what is needed, and then you can hit the target.

How can we connect with you?

Abroad Talents is a company that aims at helping talent, especially US international students and professionals, find their dream jobs in the USA.

My website is www.AbroadTalents.com, and it has a job board to let you explore thousands of jobs opportunities which support H-1B (working VISA)/OPT/OPT extension. All of the jobs on our website are H-1B supported or e-verified employers.

It is FREE to sign up to explore thousands of H-1B or OPT/OPT extension jobs.

Nailing Jobs in Any Economy & Country, with Karen Kartika

Born and raised in Indonesia, I first came to the US in 1995 for my undergraduate studies in communications, which later continued with completing my MBA in 2002.

I have held multiple jobs ever since I migrated to the US: from being an International Student Department office staff person, a program coordinator for a local TV station, and a sales pep for nationwide local TV stations, to finally establishing my career as a media strategist and executive for multinational advertising agencies with Fortune 500 companies as clients.

These were my best years learning and growing. I spent a few years in the US and Asia with this career.

But in 2011, I felt I needed a different direction and followed another passion of helping people cultivate their highest potential.

In 2012, I established myself as a coach, and now I cater my service to professionals who are seeking mid-career transitions into different fields or entrepreneurship.

What is your background in your home country?

I spent my youth in Indonesia. I'm of Chinese decent. My grandparents and great grandparents migrated from China to Indonesia.

As a third generation Chinese Indonesian, my parents insisted on keeping the Chinese tradition alive in our home, but without the language immersion, as they did not speak much of it themselves.

As a minority in my country of origin, my parents taught me the importance of assimilating, staying relevant, and preparing for the future, building relationships and connections, and bringing the best of myself despite the diversity.

What was your job-hunting experience in the US like?

When I first job hunted in the US during or after my undergraduate years (in the '90s— yikes!), I considered myself very lucky.

All of the jobs that I wanted, I nailed them. I studied mass communications, and my school (Emerson College in Boston) was well-known in the media, broadcasting, and marketing industry.

Mind you, this was pre-Internet, so I relied heavily on the job postings at my school's career center to find these jobs.

I loved working, I wanted to be someone, to have a meaningful life, and to be financially independent.

So I was determined to get a job. Period.

Even as an international student who did not have a working visa (only F1/student visa), I worked throughout my undergraduate years.

I held various jobs at school, and my favorite was working at the International Student Advisor Department.

I made lots of friends from all over the world. I helped the advisor create events and booklets.

I managed her schedules and organized her office. So before I graduated, I already had a resume as beefed up as those of the American students who had been working since high school.

I was a stickler for the rules (as much as I like to bend them at times). So when my study program called for internships, I applied for one. I always wanted to work for a TV station, so I sought the largest local TV station (WGBH Boston) and landed an internship in its programming department.

At the same time, I joined the student organization called Emerson TV. I produced a news and drama series for the school TV, and later the school's version of the Oscar, called the EVVY.

I also took a winter internship in LA—just to confirm that I would not get into the production side of the entertainment industry.

Becoming a starving editor, producer, and director was never part of my dream.

I found that side of the industry too competitive and hardcore. Being an international student with limited English, I bowed out of that dream.

When it came time for OPT, I looked for a job in the

business side of television. I got to know TV sales and advertising. I applied to a few positions and got a job at one of the largest TV sales companies, called Petry TV.

The company closed its doors recently, and the media industry has changed so much since I was there.

At that time, I did not have the intention yet to live in the US, so I was just grateful that I could complete my OPT and was ready to go home.

But in 1998–1999, my country, along with a few other Southeast Asian countries experienced great turmoil. There was a coup to bring down the president that involved creating social unrest (murders, rapes, destroying houses and buildings) which targeted the Chinese Indonesians.

Near the end of my OPT, my parents suggested that I stay longer in the US. But without a visa, I could not do so. The only way to stay was either to apply for asylum or go back to school.

I chose the latter.

At that time, Silicon Valley was starting to set its foot. Dial-up Internet providers Prodigy and Netscape (which later become AOL) were big names in tech.

I heard jobs were booming in the area, so I began my quest to look for school there.

I wanted to learn business, so an MBA was the next natural progression. I got accepted at San Jose State University and said goodbye to cold, wintery Boston.

Because of the situation that was happening to the Southeast Asian countries, the US was allowing international students from these countries to apply for jobs outside of campus to financially support their studies.

Not many students heard about this, and when they couldn't pay for their tuition, they returned to their home countries.

But not me.

Being active in the International Students Department had its plusses! I applied for this program and got a special letter to override the note on my social security as proof of my eligibility to work as a nonresident.

Again, my school's career center was my best friend. I applied to a recent job posting for a small media advertising agency in Mountain View and got accepted within a week. The owner of the company, my boss, was a well-known media strategist in the industry, and I learned so much from her.

For the next five years in San Jose (even with a short break due to going into a restaurant business with my friends), I built my career as a media buyer, researcher, and planner for many Silicon Valley companies, from start-ups to global players.

In 2004, with the change of the economic landscape, Asia was booming and becoming a goldmine for career-minded people like me.

Through connections that I gained in my five years working in Silicon Valley, I landed a job in Asia.

With hard work and networking with the right people, I climbed the corporate ladder quickly. And when it was time for me to move back to the US five years later, it was relatively easy as well because I had the credibility and the people who vouched for me.

If you could only give one piece of advice, what would you tell new immigrants to the US about the job search?

I understand that the job search landscape has changed a lot from when I started. There are more opportunities, more options, and more information about what's available and not available.

I find this to be good but also bad in the sense that it can become overwhelming and scary. I hear as a general sentiment that looking for a job is hard, that it takes a lot of effort—almost like a full-time job on its own. If you believe in this, you will project it on your path.

I invite you just to peek and look around, look at the online job sites, look at your favorite companies' websites.

There are jobs—lots of them. Yes, some of them might not be what you envision yourself doing right now (not your dream job), but why not give it a try?

The key for a newbie in any new market is to prove that you can work.

I'm not advising you to do something that's totally against your value, your purpose, or totally irrelevant to your field/expertise, but to begin, you must be willing to start somewhere.

Pick up a job that can support and connect you to your ultimate goal, whether it's a job position or a company where you want to work.

Even if you have to start with a part-time job or an internship, just do it, work hard at it, stand out from the crowd, and connect with the right people who can take you to the next level.

Focus on the goal and do whatever it takes. Support yourself with the right people because relationships and connections are essential to your success in entering and climbing the corporate ladder (or in any professional/business endeavors).

How can we connect with you?

I am a success strategist and executive coach.

I help visionaries, corporate leaders, and business owners unpack their visions and bring them to reality. There's often a big gap between a great idea and making it real and fruitful.

And this big difference comes from poor planning, lack of direction, and one's own nonsupportive habits, structures, and thought patterns. Not like other coaches, I offer a hands-on approach to my clients' career, business, and personal plans, not just pieces of advice and homework.

I combine my background in business operations, marketing, and communications, with my years practicing body and mind healing therapies, to help my clients achieve clarity and increase their creativity and productivity and create breakthroughs to their goals and success.

I can offer a FREE 30-minute strategy call for your readers. They can send me an e- mail to schedule at karenvkartika@gmail.com. I can also be found at karenvkartika.com.

From Africa to Anaheim, with Lionnel Yamentou

Born and raised in Cameroon (Central Africa), I traveled to Ghana (West Africa) for undergraduate studies, where I spent 7 years to earn that first degree.

I then started a web services business and hosted a very successful developers' conference.

In 2011, I traveled to the US for graduate studies, got a job during my first six months in my master's degree program, and am still working for that employer, 3 years after my graduation.

What is your background in your home country?

Even though my country of birth is Cameroon, I feel a stronger connection to Ghana because it is only when I left Cameroon that I was exposed to situations that challenged me to grow as a person.

In Ghana, I earned a bachelor's degree in computing and its practice from The Open University in the UK (distance learning.)

I was already interested in computers before leaving Cameroon in 2004, but that interest turned into a passion when I started studying them in detail while in Ghana.

What was your job-hunting experience in the US like?

The first year in the US was the most challenging.

Holding a student visa, I was told that even though we had the option to intern as part of the CPT option of our curriculum, I had to wait for 3 to 6 months before I could start with that.

Since my university was growing and I had noticed a few problems with the IT infrastructure, which I was qualified to solve, I decided to apply to work on campus as a tech support staff member or intern.

The director of administration told me they needed a software developer more than they needed tech support staff, and I said I could do that.

I had already worked on a few software development projects back in Ghana. He gave me a test, which I successfully completed, and about a month after my application, I was hired to work as an intern on campus, earning minimum wage.

Things have very much improved since 2012, and today my earnings and work conditions are tremendously better than what they were then.

If you could only give one piece of advice, what would you tell new immigrants to the US about the job search?

There are opportunities all around us. Never let someone else's experience (good or bad) determine what your expectations of yourself are.

You are unique, and whatever you want, which you know is best for you, is what you will get. Always expect the best for yourself, befriend people who challenge you to grow, and work diligently to achieve your set goals.

How can we connect with you?

When I am not working with computers, I enjoy helping the young and young at heart prepare for the future, so they can focus and make the most of today. My website is at www.Yamentou.com, and I am available for speaking opportunities, corporate training, and one-on-one or group coaching.?

Shanghai to New York & Beyond

I am originally from Shanghai, China.

I started my undergrad in California and then transferred to the University of Washington, double majoring in economics and applied math.

Now I am a data science grad student at Columbia University. During this summer, I am an intern at Swiss Re.

My expected graduation date is Dec 2016, so my job hunting will start soon!

What is your background in your home country?

Most of my family members work in banking and the accounting industry, so my major was finance when I started my undergrad.

But later I realized this major was not a good fit for me, so I switched to a more technical side.

What was your job hunting experience in the US like?

In general, it wasn't easy.

Between my undergrad and grad program, I had an 8-month gap (graduated in Dec 2014), so I decided to look for a temporary job.

Because I knew I would continue my studies instead of staying in a company, I did not spend too much time preparing, like thinking of answers to interview questions, practicing on LeetCode, brushing up my resume and such.

So when I went to the interview, I failed big time. ALWAYS PREPARE AND PRACTICE. They will see through you.

If you could only give one piece of advice, what would you tell new immigrants to the US about the job search?

ALWAYS PREPARE AND PRACTICE. Study the job description, even if the jobs you applied for have the same title.

Every job is different from others. And those people who focus on the difference and details are the ones get the jobs.

My Thoughts on Being an Immigrant Professional in the US:

I hope you learned a lot from everyone who shared their stories here and, if nothing else, showed that it is absolutely possible for you to land your dream job as well.

No matter what country you are from, what your English sounds like, and how little or much experience you have, you can land your dream job in the US.

CHAPTER 10: HOW TO LAND YOUR AMERICAN DREAM JOB

Hooray, you've finished the book!

I don't want you to read this book, feel good about it, then do nothing.

Whether you're a new grad looking to find your first job, or you're looking to get out of a job that you don't like that much, this book is meant to serve as a jump-off point for you to take action.

Whether it's finally finding the job title that was meant for you,

Or getting multiple interviews after many resume rejections,

Or negotiating your salary for the first time.

I hope this book has helped to point you in the direction of where you could go and expanded your vision of what is possible for you as an immigrant in the US.

Now that you know the basics of what to do, it's time to share with you HOW to do it.

The job search isn't the easiest thing in the world, and you're already ahead of 90% of job seekers who just try to wing it.

My personal philosophy is this: learn from the best.

I've put together a boot camp for you that will take you instantly from not sure how to land your dream job to getting $100,000+ jobs like my clients have.

I've created The Employed Immigrant Boot Camp, an online course that distills my 4 years of experience in my own job search and also helping many of my clients landing their dream jobs.

Visit www.EmployedImmigrant.com for more information.

ABOUT THE AUTHOR

Li Lin is a career coach who helps immigrant professionals land 6 figure jobs.

She came to the US in 2000 from Shanghai, China.

She graduated from UC Berkeley in 2012, and worked as a business analyst in San Francisco.

She currently lives in Southern California, and you can learn more about her at www.TheSuccessfulimmigrant.com

Want more?

Looking for an H-1B or OPT Job and hang out on Linkedin a lot?

Join the H-1B and OPT Immigrant Job Seekers group on Linkedin by visiting this group here:

https://www.linkedin.com/groups/7041184/

Looking to hang out with other successful immigrants on Facebook?

Join the Successful Immigrants Facebook group here:

https://www.facebook.com/groups/successfulimmigrants/

See you there!

-Li

Made in the USA
Lexington, KY
02 December 2019